My Amazing Toddler **Behavioral Series**

I Keep My Hands to Myself.

I Know MY BOUNDARIES!

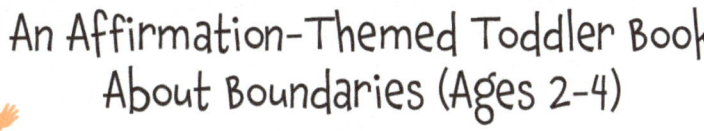

An Affirmation-Themed Toddler Book
About Boundaries (Ages 2-4)

By

Suzanne T. Christian

TWORAVENS
BOOKS

Two Little Ravens
CHILDREN'S NON-FICTION BOOKS

Paperback Edition: 9781964202174
Hardcover Edition: 9781964202181
Digital Edition: 9781964202198

Published in the United States by Two Ravens Books LLC,
254 Chapman Rd, Ste 209, Newark DE 19702

'Expand the mind, free the imagination, one title at a time.'
www.tworavensbooks.com

Welcome to
"I Keep My Hands to Myself. I Know My Boundaries!"

This book is a fun and engaging collection of simple affirmations created just for young children. As you read together, your toddler will learn the importance of respecting personal space and boundaries and understanding their needs.

Each page offers colorful illustrations and everyday situations that help gently reinforce positive behavior. By incorporating this book into your reading routine, you'll see your child's awareness of boundaries grow through repetition—a key element in early learning.

Get ready for a journey of self-awareness, respect, and much fun with your toddler!

Suzanne T. Christian

My hands are mine,
and that's just fine!

I give
big high-fives,
but I ask first.

When I need space,
I say, "Stop, please!"

I love hugs,
but I ask first.

Sometimes, we all need a little space.

When I wait in line, I keep my hands by my side.

I say,
"Can I play too?"
before I join the fun.

I jump for joy when I'm excited but in my own space!

I take a step back when
a friend needs room.

My hands are for waving, clapping, and high-fives!

When I want to sit close, I ask,
"Is this spot okay?"

Sharing is fun,
but I always
ask first,
"Can we share?"

I can be close,
but not too close.
I know my boundaries!

Yes!

When I ask,
sometimes I hear "**yes**,"
and sometimes I hear "**no**,"
and that's okay!

When a friend
says "**no**,"
I listen and give
them space—
I am kind!

NO!

Stop means
STOP!

I can play
and still give
space—yay!

I'm kind when I give my friends space!

"Please don't touch!" keeps me and my friends safe!

I keep my hands
to myself when
waiting in line—
it's my secret
power!

I respect my space,
and I respect yours too!

I keep my hands to myself.
I know my boundaries!
The End!

My Amazing Toddler Behavioral Series

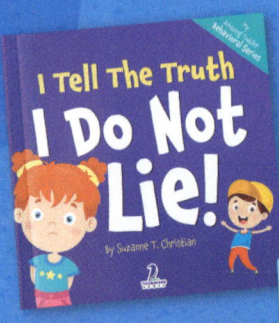
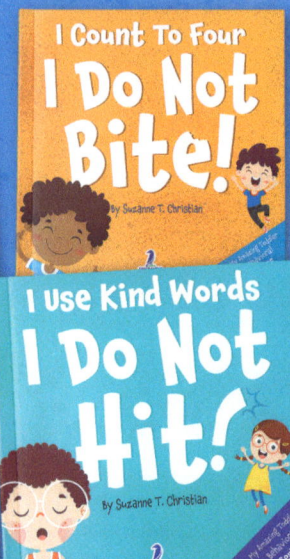
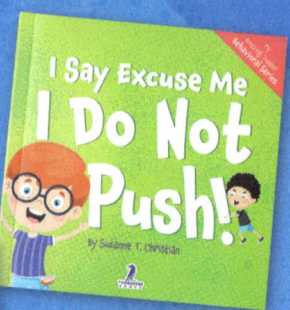
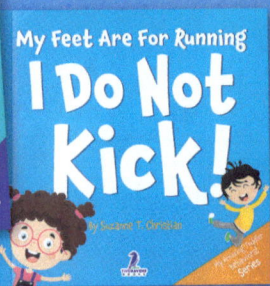

Check Out
Suzanne T. Christian's beloved series
'My Amazing Toddler Behavioral Series'.
Young readers are sure to enjoy!

Two Little Ravens
CHILDREN'S NON-FICTION BOOKS

Dear Amazing Reader,

Thank you for diving into **I Keep My Hands to Myself. I Know My Boundaries!** with me. If this book touched your heart or made a difference for a young reader, I'd be grateful if you could share your thoughts in a review. Your feedback inspires my future work and helps others discover the magic within these pages.

I'd love to hear from you directly if you have suggestions or ideas for improving the book. Please feel free to reach out to me at **suzanne.christian@tworavensbooks.com.** Your voice counts, and I cherish it deeply.

With heartfelt gratitude,

www.ingramcontent.com/pod-product-compliance
Lightning Source LLC
Chambersburg PA
CBHW041559120626
46551CB00002B/264